Freedom Fighters

Martin Luther King, Jr.

Mark Falstein

Globe Fearon Educational Publisher
Paramus, New Jersey

Paramount Publishing

Freedom Fighters

Cesar Chavez

Fannie Lou Hamer

Martin Luther King, Jr.

Malcolm X

Nelson Mandela

Excerpts from speeches beginning on pages 12, 36, and 68 reprinted by arrangement with The Heirs to the Estate of Martin Luther King, Jr., c/o Joan Daves Agency as agent for the proprietor.

I Have a Dream: Copyright 1963 by Martin Luther King, Jr., copyright renewed 1991 by Coretta Scott King. *I've Been to the Mountaintop:* Copyright 1968 the Estate of Martin Luther King, Jr. *Rosa Parks:* Copyright 1955 by Martin Luther King, Jr., copyright renewed 1983 by Coretta Scott King.

We Shall Overcome, page 23.
Musical and Lyrical Adaptation by Zilphia Horton, Frank Hamilton, Guy Carawan, and Pete Seger. Inspired by African American Gospel Singing Members of the Food and Tobacco Workers Union, Charleston, SC, and the southern Civil Rights Movement.
TRO © copyright 1960 (renewed 1988) and 1963 (renewed 1991) Ludlow Music, Inc., New York, NY
Royalties derived from this composition are being contributed to the We Shall Overcome Fund and The Freedom Movement under the trusteeship of the writers. Used by Permission

Editor: Sharon Wheeler
Production editor: Joe C. Shines
Cover and text design: London Road Design
Production: ExecuStaff

Photographs: Cover, pp. 16, 25, 42, 53, 70—UPI/Bettmann Newsphotos; pg. 35—The Bettmann Archive

ISBN 0–8224–3220–X

Printed in the United States of America

4. 10 9 8 7 6 5 4 3 2 1
MA

Contents

CHAPTER 1

A Preacher's Son from Atlanta

Later, he would remember that Sunday in 1949 as the day his life changed.

The hall was crowded. The people had come to hear a talk by Dr. Mordecai Johnson, the president of Howard University. Dr. Johnson had just returned from a trip to India. His subject was the Indian freedom fighter, Mahatma Gandhi. Dr. Johnson described Gandhi's methods of nonviolent protest that led to India's independence from Britain. Listening closely to his words was a young seminary student from Georgia named Martin Luther King, Jr.

Martin had often heard Gandhi mentioned as an example of how black people in America might win their struggle for equality. Yet the young man was doubtful. Strikes, boycotts, and protest marches may have worked in India, he had always thought, but not here. The descendants of African slaves in America suffered far more cruelty than the Indians under the British.

Young Martin, or "M. L." as he was called then, was a student at Crozer Theological Seminary. As a Christian minister, he believed in Jesus's teaching that one should "love one's enemies." It was a fine way for individuals to deal with one another, but for an entire race? Still, he knew that violence against white power was not only foolish, it was morally wrong. He had struggled to overcome his own hate and anger toward white people. For years he had asked himself what the role of the church should be in fighting racism. He had read the books of the great thinkers, talked for hours with his professors, and searched his own heart without coming up with an answer.

Now listening to Dr. Johnson, he thought he might have found one.

Martin Luther King, Jr., was born in Atlanta, Georgia, on January 15, 1929. From an early age, he'd been expected to become a preacher. He had a way with words, and he came from a family in which religion was important. M. L., his sister Christine, and his brother A. D., read aloud from the Bible every day. His grandmother entertained them with Bible stories. His grandfather, the Reverend

Adam Daniel Williams, had founded Atlanta's Ebenezer Baptist Church. His father, the Reverend Martin Luther King, Sr., had married Williams's daughter, Alberta, and followed him as pastor at Ebenezer. Under "Daddy King," it had become one of Atlanta's leading black churches.

Of course, no white Baptist ever attended Ebenezer. Like every southern community, Atlanta lived under the rule of "Jim Crow." This was a slang term for segregation—a system of laws that kept white and black citizens separate and unequal. The two races lived in separate areas of town. They sat in separate sections in buses, railroad cars, and theaters. There were Jim Crow restaurants, hospitals, hotels, parks, rest rooms, and drinking fountains. Each displayed a sign reading WHITES ONLY or COLORED ONLY.

Those places set aside for "the colored" were always older and shabbier. In most stores, African American customers had to use rear entrances. They were kept waiting until all the white customers had been served. Black children attended separate schools, where they rarely got the education available to whites. Most Southern blacks were denied even the most basic right of citizens—the right to vote.

Any protest against this system was met by white violence. Terrorist groups like the Ku Klux Klan threatened and beat up blacks. They burned their houses and sometimes killed those who fought back. Blacks were hanged for such crimes as "insulting a white person."

Rarely were whites punished for violence against blacks. The police all were white. The judges and juries all were white. The government officials all were white.

The Kings wanted to protect their children from the pain of racism. But they could not. When Martin was five, his closest friend was a white boy. One day his friend's parents told him that he could no longer play with their son. "But why?" he asked, puzzled. "Because we are white and you are colored," he was told.

As he grew up, Martin always remembered a lesson his father taught him about dealing with racism: "You must never feel that you are less than anyone else. You must always feel that you are *somebody*." He remembered it when he learned that white people called his neighborhood "nigger town." He remembered it when he saw white police officers beating up black children. He remembered it when a white woman slapped him and called him "a little nigger."

When he was in the eleventh grade, Martin won first prize in a speech contest. It was held in a distant town. That evening, he was returning to Atlanta by bus with his teacher. At one town, some white people got on and could find no seats. The driver ordered M. L. and his teacher to give up theirs. M. L. refused. The driver cursed and threatened him. Finally, at his teacher's pleading, he got up and stood the rest of the way home. "That night will never leave my mind," he said many years later. "It was the angriest I had ever been in my life." His parents understood his anger, but they told him that it was his Christian duty to love whites. "How can I love a race of people who hate me?" he snapped back.

Despite his anger, Martin continued to do well in high school. At the age of 15, he entered Morehouse College. Morehouse was one of the leading black colleges in the South. Dr. Benjamin Mays, the college president, was a teacher he came to admire greatly. Dr. Mays was an educated and religious African American who was not afraid to speak out against injustice.

But it was at Morehouse that Martin had his first positive contacts with white people. In his senior year, M. L. was chosen to serve on the Atlanta Intercollegiate Council. Here he met students from all over the city—including white students. "As I got to see more of white people," he later remembered, "my resentment softened and a spirit of cooperation took its place." When blacks and whites could meet on fairly equal terms, he discovered, there was little room for anger. At the same time, his professors were leading him to see that racism, not white people, was the enemy. They encouraged him to look for positive solutions to racism.

Martin realized that he could not sit back while other people worked for those solutions. He had thought about becoming a doctor or lawyer, but now he knew that his place was in the church. He had already preached his first sermon at Ebenezer. At the age of 18, he was ordained as a minister and became assistant pastor of his father's church. When he graduated from Morehouse in 1948, he chose to study for a degree in divinity. He was accepted at Crozer Theological Seminary in Pennsylvania—far from his family and far from the South.

Crozer was a far different world than Morehouse. There were fewer than 100 students, and only twelve of them were African American. There was racism and poverty in Pennsylvania, but there were no Jim Crow laws. Martin knew that racist whites thought of blacks as lazy, careless people who never took anything seriously. It embarrassed him if he was a minute late to class or his shoes weren't polished. No one would ever call M. L. King lazy or careless! He earned straight A's. He took the train to Philadelphia for special classes in philosophy. He talked far into the night with his professors and other students.

The more he read, the more he believed that being a Christian meant working for the freedom of all people. Human beings were basically good, M. L. believed. They might be cruel to each other, but they had the power to improve themselves. The church must lead in bringing about this improvement. A religion had to fight the evils of poverty and injustice. But what was the right way for the church to fight?

After Dr. Johnson's talk, Martin went to a bookstore and bought six books about Gandhi. He found that

Gandhi, like himself, had to overcome hate and anger in his life. Gandhi's way was not for cowards. His people had defeated evil by *refusing to go along with it.* Here was the answer Martin had been searching for. This was how "loving one's enemies" could win freedom for his people. Jesus had given him the spirit; now Gandhi had shown him the way.

It was not an easy or popular way. Gandhi himself had been murdered by an Indian who resented his program of freedom for all religions. And the fear and hatred between black and white Americans was much older and stronger than that between the Indians and the British. But through courage, love, and truth, it could be overcome.

"The chain of hatred must be cut," Martin told himself. "Only then can brotherhood begin."

It was a strong chain, and the first blow would have to be strong.

CHAPTER 2

"Don't Ride the Bus Today!"

Rosa Parks's feet were sore. She had been standing all day at her job sewing clothes in a department store. As she waited for the bus, she was looking forward to sitting down. It was Thursday, December 1, 1955, in Montgomery, Alabama.

On Montgomery's buses, the first four rows were reserved for whites. The back was for blacks. And there was a middle section that blacks could use as long as no white people wanted it. If the front filled up and a white person wanted a seat in the middle, the black person had to move to the back.

When the bus arrived, the "colored" section was full. Rosa Parks took a seat in the middle. A few stops later, some white people boarded the bus. They filled up the front section, and one man was left standing. The driver turned around. "All right, I need those middle seats," he said.

The people in the middle section didn't move.

This time, the driver's voice carried a threat. "You all better make it light on yourselves and let me have those seats," he said.

With a sigh, the man next to Rosa Parks stood and moved to the back of the bus. Two women also left their seats. But Mrs. Parks slid over and took the man's seat by the window.

The driver stared at her. "Are you going to stand up?" he demanded.

All Rosa Parks wanted was to go home and get her dinner. But she was tired, and she saw no reason why she should have to stand.

"No, I'm not," she said.

"If you don't stand up, I'm going to have you arrested," the driver said.

"Then go on and have me arrested," she replied.

Coretta Scott King answered the telephone. "Martin, it's for you," she called to her husband.

"Martin?" said the man on the phone. "This is E. D. Nixon. A woman who used to work for me was arrested last night for refusing to give up her seat on a bus."

"Yes, I heard about it," Martin Luther King said. "Rosa Parks." King knew that Nixon ran the Montgomery office of the NAACP—the National Association for the Advancement of Colored People. Since 1909, this organization had been using the courts to fight for the civil rights of African Americans.

"We're going to challenge the bus segregation law," Nixon said. "But I'm also trying to organize a one-day boycott as a protest. I want to urge all blacks to stay off the buses this Monday."

"Have you called Ralph Abernathy?" King asked. The Reverend Abernathy was one of Montgomery's leading black ministers and Martin's best friend.

"Yes, I just spoke to him," Nixon said. "We're setting up a meeting of community leaders tonight, people who can make sure the boycott doesn't get violent. We'd especially like ministers to spread the word in their churches on Sunday. Can we count on you?"

"Of course," King said. "In fact, if you need a place for your meeting, you can use my church."

The last four years had been happy ones for Martin Luther King, Jr. Just two weeks earlier, his wife, Coretta, had given birth to their first child, a girl named Yolanda Denise. Martin had met Coretta Scott in Boston, where she was studying music. At first Coretta wasn't sure she wanted a life as a "preacher's wife," but she soon learned that Martin was no ordinary preacher. They were married in June 1953.

Meanwhile, Martin was completing his studies at Boston University. He earned the degree of Doctor of Divinity. Even before he finished school, he'd had several job offers. He'd thought of becoming a pastor in Detroit or teaching at a college. Dr. Mays had offered him a job at Morehouse. But he chose to move to Montgomery and become the pastor of Dexter Avenue Baptist Church.

Coretta had gone along with this decision, but not happily. She was from a small town in Alabama. She wanted to live in the North so their children could get a better education and not have to grow up living under the Jim Crow system. Martin also had second thoughts about the job. But the South was his home and Coretta's too. And as a pastor, he would be better able to help African Americans in their struggle for equality.

Early on the following Monday morning, December 5, Coretta excitedly called Martin to the window. A bus was rumbling down the street. At that hour, the buses were usually jammed with people. This one was empty. The next bus was empty too. The third carried only two passengers, both white.

Dr. King got in his car and drove around the city to check out the bus routes. He counted only eight black passengers. The community was supporting the boycott!

That afternoon, there was a meeting of community leaders. They called for a meeting that evening to urge people to continue the boycott until bus segregation was ended and African American drivers were hired. The group chose Martin as their president. He was only 26 and did not see himself as a leader. He guessed that he had been chosen because he hadn't been in Montgomery long and "hadn't had time to make any enemies." Whatever the reason, he had to make a speech at that evening's meeting.

There were TV cameras and reporters at the Holt Street Baptist Church. It was so crowded that thousands of people had to stand outside. They cheered when Rosa Parks was introduced. Dr. King talked about her case and others. Every person at the meeting had experienced something like what had happened to Mrs. Parks.

"You know, my friends," Dr. King said, "there comes a time when people get tired of being trampled by the brutal feet of oppression. There comes a time, my friends, when people get tired of . . . humiliation. We are here this evening because we are tired *now!*"

There were shouts of "Amen!" and "Say it, brother!" as at a Sunday morning church service.

"We had no alternative but to protest," Dr. King went on. "For many years we have shown amazing patience. We have sometimes given our white brothers the feeling that we like the way we are being treated. But we come here tonight to be saved from that patience that makes us patient with anything less than freedom and justice!

"Now, let us say that we are not calling for violence. We have overcome that. I want it known throughout Montgomery and throughout this nation that we are a Christian people. We believe in the teachings of Jesus. The only weapon we have in our hands is the weapon of protest. We are protesting for the birth of justice in our community. . . . We will be guided by the highest principles of law and order. In spite of our mistreatment, we must not become bitter and end up by hating our white brothers . . ."

The next day, the name of Martin Luther King, Jr., was on the front page of newspapers across America.

The bus boycott continued. All over Montgomery, people pitched in to help. Car pools were set up. Drivers offered rides to strangers. Black-owned taxi companies charged their customers only ten cents a ride. But most people walked miles every day to get to work.

Dr. King met with bus company officials and city leaders. They talked back and forth about the boycotters' demands. The bus company felt that if it gave in, the city's African Americans would brag about having won a victory. And this, they felt, must not happen.

Dr. King and the other leaders of the boycott never talked about Gandhi. Their guiding idea was "Christian love." But a minister from Texas, the Reverend Glenn Smiley, understood what King was doing. Smiley led a group called the Congress of Racial Equality (CORE). They had been using Gandhi's method to fight racism since 1942. They called it "nonviolent direct action." Smiley was one of several white ministers who had come to Montgomery to help organize the boycott. Other whites gave blacks rides to and from work. Still, there were others who secretly believed that segregation was wrong but were afraid to act or to speak up.

There was reason to be afraid.

The white racists of Montgomery had begun to strike back. A group called the White Citizens' Council tried to turn black ministers against the boycott. When that failed, they spread a rumor that Dr. King had stolen money raised to support the boycott. They told the newspapers that King had called off the boycott. The stories were quickly proven to be false.

Then the police started arresting car-pool drivers—for speeding, for blocking traffic, for "operating a transport system without a license." Many drivers stopped sharing rides. They were afraid that they'd lose their driver's licenses. Martin Luther King himself was taken to jail—for going five miles an hour over the speed limit.

On January 30, Dr. King was at a meeting when someone threw a bomb on the front porch of his house. Coretta and the baby were in a back room with a friend, or they might have been killed. Martin and the other leaders had received letters and phone calls threatening violence almost every day. Now someone had followed through on the threat.

When Martin arrived home, he found a very angry group of his friends and supporters outside. The house was full of police. After making sure his family was safe, he stood on the burned porch and spoke to the crowd. "If you have weapons, take them home," he said. "If you do not have them, please do not seek to get them. We cannot solve this problem through violence. We must meet violence with nonviolence."

There was no further trouble in Montgomery that evening.

There would, however, be more threats and more bombings. The city and the bus company tried one means after another to stop the boycott. But Dr. King held it together for nearly a year.

Then on November 13, 1956, the United States Supreme Court ruled in the case brought by the NAACP. Alabama's bus segregation laws were declared unconstitutional. The black community had won.

The court order reached Montgomery on December 20. That evening, Dr. King told a cheering crowd, "It is my firm conviction that God is working in Montgomery. Let all men of goodwill, both black and white, continue to work with him."

The next day a group of community leaders boarded a bus together. They included Dr. King, Rosa Parks,

A year after she was arrested for performing this same act, Rosa Parks sat freely in the front of a bus in Montgomery. In 1956, the U.S. Supreme Court declared the city's bus segregation laws unconstitutional.

E. D. Nixon, Ralph Abernathy, and the white minister Glenn Smiley. There was no trouble. It looked as though Montgomery would peacefully accept the end of Jim Crow, at least on buses. Blacks in other southern cities began protests against segregation laws.

But soon after, a black teenage girl was dragged off a bus and beaten. Other buses were shot at. Two weeks later, three African American churches and Ralph Abernathy's home were bombed, and a wave of terror began to spread across the South.

CHAPTER 3

The Movement

There were some white southerners who hated blacks and thought they were less than human. There were others who feared that if white people didn't stay "on top," blacks would "take over." There were still others who were afraid they might lose their jobs if "the colored" were given an equal chance. And there were many who simply were uncomfortable with change.

But change was happening. All across the South, African Americans were standing up for their rights. Their struggle was called the civil rights movement, the freedom movement, or simply the movement. The Montgomery bus boycott had made Dr. King the country's best-known black leader. "He didn't *tell* us how to get free, he *showed* us how to get free," said one young follower. King was flooded with requests for speaking engagements. People had heard his speeches on television and were impressed by the power of his words.

In January 1957, King met with African American ministers from across the South. They formed the Southern Christian Leadership Conference (SCLC). Its aim was to fight racist laws through direct action while the NAACP fought them through the courts. King was chosen to lead the SCLC. Meanwhile, he was writing a book about the boycott and trying to find time for his church and his family.

In September 1957, the nation focused its attention on Central High School in Little Rock, Arkansas, one of the best public schools in the South. It had, as one African American student later remembered, "five floors of opportunities." In 1954, the Supreme Court had ruled that segregation in public schools was unconstitutional. The court ordered that schools be desegregated. Some communities accepted this ruling, but others, such as Little Rock, had resisted. The NAACP had finally won a court ruling to desegregate the school. Nine black teenagers were to begin classes September 4.

Early that morning, eight of them met at the home of Daisy Bates, president of the Little Rock NAACP. A group of ministers were there to drive them to school. When they got there, the building was surrounded by a white mob. Armed men blocked the doors. Governor Orville Faubus had called out the National Guard to keep the African American students from entering the school, "for their own protection." They were turned back as the mob shouted.

One student had missed the meeting. Elizabeth Eckford had not heard about the plan to go to Central in a group. She arrived at the opposite side of the school. A line of National Guardsmen drove her back with bayonets. "Nigger!" the mob screamed. "Kill her!" "Lynch her!" Then a woman broke through the mob and led Elizabeth to safety.

Every day, the "Little Rock Nine" met at Mrs. Bates's house for the ride to school. Every day, they were turned away. On September 14, Governor Faubus met with President Dwight D. Eisenhower. The president asked him to use the National Guard to enforce the court order. Faubus's response came a week later. He removed the National Guard from the school completely. The African American students were left at the mercy of the mob.

The president moved swiftly. He federalized the Arkansas National Guard, placing it directly under his command. He sent in the U.S. Army. On September 25, the nine black students finally started classes—under army protection.

Martin Luther King hoped that Little Rock might prove to be "a blessing in disguise." Whites would see that the problem of racism had to be faced directly and honestly. But it didn't happen that way. Most white Americans didn't think the rights of African Americans were important. Eisenhower had sent troops to Little Rock, but he had no interest in making civil rights a national policy.

"[He] could not be committed to anything which involved a structural change in . . . American society," Dr. King said bitterly.

In September 1958, Dr. King and his wife were in a Montgomery courthouse where Ralph Abernathy was involved in a case. A guard refused to let him enter the courtroom. When King asked to speak to Abernathy's lawyer, two policemen seized him and dragged him to jail. They beat him, choked him, and threw him into a cell.

When the police discovered that the man they were holding was Martin Luther King, they realized they had made a mistake. A photographer had taken pictures of the two officers twisting King's arms. The story made headlines. It was clear that this was the way African Americans were treated in Alabama every day. The police commissioner made no apologies. He ordered King held for trial.

This was not the first time Dr. King had been arrested for his activities. His supporters had always bailed him out. But now, he said, "the time has come when I should no longer accept bail. If I commit a crime in the name of civil rights, I will go to jail and serve the time."

"This is not the life I expected to lead," he told his friends. "If anyone had told me . . . that I would have been in this position, I would have avoided it . . . But gradually you take some responsibility, and then a little more, until finally you are not in control any more. Then, once you make up your mind . . . you are prepared to do anything that serves the cause and advances the movement."

A judge found Dr. King guilty of refusing to obey a police officer. He was ordered to pay ten dollars or serve 14 days in jail. He chose jail. He would not pay a fine for an act he did not commit. He told the court, "The brutality inflicted upon blacks has become America's shame. Last month, in Mississippi, a sheriff, who was pointed out by four eyewitnesses as the man who beat a black to death . . . was freed in 23 minutes. At this very moment in this state [a black man] sits in the death house . . . for stealing less than two dollars. Can anyone . . . believe that a *white man* could be condemned to death in Alabama for stealing this small amount?"

The police commissioner called Dr. King's statement a "publicity stunt." He paid King's fine to avoid having to jail him. Meanwhile, the conscience of America was about to be startled into wakefulness.

For several years the SCLC, CORE, and other groups had quietly been training college students in nonviolent protest. In 1959, they chose Nashville, Tennessee, as a "target city." Nashville had integrated schools and buses. There were African Americans on the school board, the city council, and the police force. But Jim Crow ruled the city's libraries, restaurants, theaters, and hotels.

Throughout the fall, students in Nashville trained at weekly meetings led by a man named Jim Lawson. He had been to India and studied the work of Gandhi. The students' "weapon" would be the *sit-in*. They would sit down in a segregated place and refuse to leave. They expected to be arrested and beaten. At their meetings they practiced protecting themselves without striking back. Through their nonviolent dignity, they hoped to shame white America into seeing the justice of their cause.

As it turned out, the sit-ins began not in Nashville but in Greensboro, North Carolina. On February 1, 1960, four black college students sat down at a segregated lunch counter. They were refused service. The next day two other students joined them. Within two weeks, sit-ins were taking place in four states.

In April, Ella Baker, an SCLC leader, helped the students set up their own organization, the Student Nonviolent Coordinating Committee, or SNCC. By the end of the year, they had held sit-ins in more than 100 cities and towns. They boycotted segregated businesses. They marched through the streets in protest against white violence, chanting "Freedom now!" They sang "We Shall Overcome," the song that had become the anthem of the movement:

> *We shall overcome, we shall overcome,*
> *We shall overcome some day.*
> *Deep in my heart I do believe*
> *We shall overcome some day.*©

In many places, police stood aside and let lawless whites beat and torture the protesters. People poured hot coffee over the protesters' heads. They dropped lighted cigarettes on their clothes. Then the police would move in and arrest the protesters. But the students would not respond with violence. Many of them carried cards that read "Remember the teachings of Jesus Christ, Mahatma Gandhi, and Martin Luther King."

Dr. King was now living in Atlanta. He had become co-pastor with his father at Ebenezer Baptist Church. On October 19, 1960, SNCC students in Atlanta got him to join in one of their sit-ins. It was at a restaurant in a department store. King and 35 others were arrested. Because earlier in the year King had been arrested for driving with an invalid license, county officials said he had now violated probation. King was sentenced to six months' hard labor in the state penitentiary.

The sentence shocked the country. Many people had come to admire the students' courage. Everyone knew their protests weren't about lunch counters—they were about freedom, dignity, and equality. Though Dr. King was not a part of their group, he was widely viewed as the national leader of the movement.

No one was more worried than Coretta Scott King. As her husband sat in jail, she received a phone call. "Hello, Mrs. King?" Coretta caught her breath. The voice on the other end was one she'd been hearing almost every night

Four college students took part in the first sit-in at a segregated lunch counter in Greensboro, North Carolina.

on television that year. "This is Senator Kennedy, and I'm calling to let you know I was thinking about you. I understand you are expecting a baby."

John F. Kennedy was the Democratic party's candidate for president of the United States. The election was less than two weeks away. Dr. King knew about Kennedy and had even met him. Frankly, King had not been impressed by the senator's civil rights voting record. Kennedy seemed too anxious about losing the votes of southern whites.

Of course, Coretta knew someone must have told him about her family, but she was pleased by his personal touch. "I know this must be very hard for you," Kennedy said. "If there's any way I can help, please feel free to call on me."

Coretta thanked him. "If there is anything you can do," she said, "I would deeply appreciate it."

That evening, Robert Kennedy, the candidate's brother and campaign manager, called the judge in Georgia and asked him why Dr. King could not be released on bail. The judge changed his mind and King was released the next day.

African American voters took notice. On election day, they turned out in record numbers to vote for "the man who got Dr. King out of jail." Kennedy narrowly won the election. At last, many blacks thought, we might have a president who is committed to "liberty and justice for *all*." It looked as though the year 1961 might bring real change.

CHAPTER 4

"Freedom Now!"

The first test of the new president's commitment came in May 1961. By federal law, there was not supposed to be segregation on buses that traveled between states. But Jim Crow, not the U.S. Constitution, was the law in most southern states. James Farmer, the leader of CORE, planned a "sit-in on wheels." He chose groups of blacks and whites trained in nonviolence to ride buses across the South. If anyone tried to stop them, the president would have to enforce the law.

The first "freedom riders," seven blacks and six whites, left Washington, D.C., on May 4. They planned to travel south to Atlanta, then west across Alabama and Mississippi to New Orleans, Louisiana. In Atlanta, the riders had dinner with Dr. King. He told them that SCLC ministers would be available along the route to help.

On May 14, the first bus reached Anniston, Alabama. A group of six Klansmen came on board. They beat the white riders and threw the blacks into the back of the bus. In Birmingham, the bus was met by a mob. There was not a police officer in sight. The freedom riders were beaten with pipes and dumped in an alley.

The second bus never reached Birmingham. When it pulled into Anniston, it too was surrounded by an armed mob. Someone cut the tires. Others held the door closed, broke a window, and tossed in a bomb. The riders barely managed to escape. The next day, another mob blocked the bus station in Birmingham and stopped the ride from going on.

In Nashville, leaders of SNCC felt that the freedom rides could not stop now. If they did, racists would think that nonviolent African Americans and other members of the movement would always give in to violence. The movement would be finished. Dozens of students volunteered to continue the freedom rides. Some left sealed letters in the SNCC office to be mailed to their loved ones if they were killed.

Law and order had broken down in Alabama. White mobs beat freedom riders with baseball bats. They attacked news reporters and burned their cars. Police arrested the riders, took them out of jail at night and dumped them on lonely country roads.

On May 21, a rally in support of the riders was held at Ralph Abernathy's church in Montgomery. As Martin Luther King spoke, a mob formed outside the church. They set a car on fire. Then they attacked the church itself. They threw rocks through the windows. As the people inside huddled together, King found his way to the basement and phoned Robert Kennedy.

The president's brother was now the United States attorney general. He was in charge of all federal law enforcement. For months the movement had been waiting for the president to take a stand for civil rights. They had been bitterly disappointed. The attorney general had tried to get the governor of Alabama to protect the riders. Now Dr. King told Robert Kennedy that a mob was about to burn down the church. The attorney general told him that federal marshals were on their way. When King looked out the window, he saw the uniformed marshals fighting hand-to-hand with the mob. King and the others stayed in the church praying until the battle was over and the streets were cleared.

President John Kennedy still would not commit himself to civil rights. Robert Kennedy even tried to persuade James Farmer to stop the freedom rides. They were embarrassing the president, he said. "Doesn't [he] know that we've been embarrassed all our lives?" responded Ralph Abernathy.

The freedom rides continued. Martin Luther King wrote admiringly of the students' willingness "to fill the jails as if they were honors classes." Through the sit-ins and freedom rides, they were breaking down the barriers of segregation.

Meanwhile, Dr. King was working with the SCLC in what he thought was the most important battle of the civil rights struggle: winning the right to vote. He was having little success. Only 29 percent of eligible southern blacks were registered to vote. In Alabama, the figure was less than 14 percent; in Mississippi, less than 5. This was largely due to the threat of white violence. In addition, many African Americans could see no point in voting. Hadn't they turned out in record numbers to elect John Kennedy? And for what? Why should they risk their lives for something so useless? King tried to convince the president that racism was a danger to the country and had to be dealt with. He urged him to issue a "second Emancipation Proclamation," to support true freedom for blacks 100 years after Lincoln had freed the slaves. But it was clear that the federal government would not act unless it was pressured.

And so the movement kept up the pressure. Civil rights leaders chose Albany, Georgia, as the target of an all-out campaign against Jim Crow. In 1961 and 1962, Albany was the scene of dozens of sit-ins. People marched through the streets in mass protests against segregation. Hundreds were jailed, Dr. King among them.

The sit-ins and protest marches did not end racism in Albany. Few African Americans became voters. Four black churches were blown up by the Ku Klux Klan. But the campaign had brought about a change in the movement. It was no longer a movement of ministers and students—thousands of ordinary people had taken part. The presence of Dr. King had brought the world's attention to Albany. The world saw a people who were no longer willing to be second-class citizens.

In Albany, the movement's leaders had learned the value of planning. They realized they had "spread themselves too thin" by going up against every target they could find. Now the SCLC decided to "hit racism in the pocket." They would choose one city with a large black population and publicly confront white power. They would do it through a boycott of segregated businesses. The country would see what it meant to be African American in the South.

The city they chose was Birmingham, Alabama. The year was 1963.

The Reverend Fred Shuttlesworth had been leading the fight against segregation in Birmingham for years. But he asked Dr. King to lead the boycott because of his national fame. The leaders of the city's African American community worked with the SCLC to organize the people. They asked blacks to boycott downtown stores. Dr. King would lead protest marches until the stores hired African American workers and a committee of both races was formed to work out a plan to end Jim Crow in Birmingham.

Birmingham's Commissioner of Public Safety, Eugene "Bull" Connor, had the protest marchers arrested, but the police guarded them against mob violence. Then Connor got a court order to stop the marches. This was something new. The movement had always had the courts on their side. Dr. King had never gone against a court order. But he had expected this moment. As Gandhi had done, he was prepared to break the law. On April 12, King and Abernathy led a group of 53 marchers toward downtown Birmingham. They were jailed for going against the court order.

In his famous "Letter from a Birmingham Jail," King wrote "an unjust law is no law at all. It is better to go to jail with dignity than to accept segregation in humility. . . . We will reach the goal of freedom in Birmingham and all over the nation, because the goal of America is freedom."

After King was released, a new plan for the demonstrations was formed. Birmingham's black high school students would be sent to desegregate public parks and libraries. On May 2, nearly 1,000 students were arrested as they marched and sang "We Shall Overcome." The next day, an even larger group of students marched. Bull Connor ordered the fire department to turn their hoses on them. The students were knocked to the ground by the force of the water.

Other African Americans, watching from across the street, were not part of Dr. King's group. They began throwing rocks and bottles at the police. Connor responded by turning police dogs loose against the marchers. Television cameras recorded the scene, and horrified Americans watched the violence on the news that evening.

The marches continued, and so did the violence. More than 2,500 protesters were beaten and dragged away to jail. On May 11, a bomb destroyed Dr. King's motel room. Another bomb blew up the home of his brother, A. D. King, now a minister in Birmingham. Angry blacks burned and looted white-owned businesses. Alabama Governor George Wallace ordered state troopers to Birmingham. President Kennedy ordered the army to stand by.

King and Abernathy made the rounds of the city's bars and pool rooms. They sought out the young African Americans who had turned to violence. They urged them to think about what they were doing. The bombings, they said, had been meant to cause just that type of reaction. The world was watching, Dr. King reminded them. A trap of violence was being set, and they shouldn't fall into it.

The violence eased off. Dr. King and SCLC leaders met with a group of Birmingham businessmen. A settlement was reached. It was agreed there would be: no segregation at lunch counters, rest rooms, fitting rooms, or drinking fountains; hiring without regard to color; help from city officials in releasing jailed marchers; and a committee of both blacks and whites to discuss problems.

The world was indeed watching in 1963. It saw African Americans marching nonviolently for their rights across the South. It saw police beating them back with hoses, sticks, electric cattle prods. That year there were more than 900 demonstrations in more than 100 cities. At the same time, movement leaders were making plans for one huge protest march on August 28—on the United States Capitol in Washington, D.C.—the "March on Washington."

After the trouble in Birmingham, President Kennedy finally began to make civil rights a national issue. He asked Congress to pass a new law. It was the most far-reaching civil rights bill ever offered by any president. It would ban all segregation in public facilities and all racial discrimination in schools, housing, and jobs. Kennedy met with civil rights leaders and tried to get them to call off the March on Washington. He was afraid the march would hurt the bill's chances to become law. The leaders refused. They would be marching for much more than the president's bill. They would be marching to show America the power of nonviolence and their determination to be free and equal citizens.

More than 250,000 people, white and black, marched in Washington that day. There was no trouble. It was, as one movement leader put it, "a great big Sunday school picnic." After the march, the people gathered at the

As a climax to the historic civil rights March on Washington, Martin Luther King delivered his "I Have a Dream" speech.

Washington Monument for a rally. Many stirring speeches were given that day, but the one that everyone remembered was Martin Luther King's.

"I say to you today, my friends, so even though we face the difficulties of today and tomorrow, I still have a dream. It is a dream deeply rooted in the American dream.

I have a dream that one day this nation will rise up and live out the true meaning of its creed: . . . that all men are created equal. I have a dream that one day . . . sons of former slaves and the sons of former slave owners will be able to sit down together at the table of brotherhood.

I have a dream that one day even the state of Mississippi . . . will be transformed into an oasis of freedom and justice.

I have a dream that my four little children will one day live in a nation where they will not be judged by the color of their skin but by the content of their character.

I have a dream today!

I have a dream that one day down in Alabama . . . little black boys and black girls will be able to join hands with little white boys and white girls and walk together as sisters and brothers.

I have a dream today!

I have a dream that one day every valley shall be exalted and every hill and mountain shall be made low. The rough places will be made plains and the crooked places will be made straight. . . .

With this faith . . . we will be able to work together, to pray together, to struggle together, to go to jail together, to stand up for freedom together, knowing that we will be free one day. . . . And if America is to be a great nation, this must become true . . .

When we let freedom ring, when we let it ring from every village and every hamlet, from every state and every city, we will be able to speed up that day when all God's children, black men and white men, Jews and gentiles, Protestants and Catholics, will be able to join hands and sing in the words of the old Negro spiritual: 'Free at last! Free at last! Thank God Almighty, we are free at last!'"

CHAPTER 5
Fighting for a Dream

Not everyone shared Dr. King's dream.

During the campaign in Birmingham, the rallying point for the marches had been the Sixteenth Street Baptist Church. On September 15, 1963, just 18 days after the March on Washington, a bomb blew apart the basement of the church. Four young girls in a Bible class were killed.

Earlier that summer, civil rights leader Medgar Evers was murdered in Jackson, Mississippi. He was shot in the back as he walked from his car to his front door.

In Georgia, a letter to a newspaper suggested that what the South needed was for someone to "shoot Martin Luther King."

Dr. King had been aware for some time that his role in the movement could mean his death. In 1958, he had barely survived an attempt on his life. He was in a bookstore in New York, signing copies of his book *Stride*

Toward Freedom. A black woman stabbed him, shouting, "Luther King, I've been after you for five years." The woman was reported to be crazy. No one knew why she hated Dr. King. The weapon almost cut an artery and might have killed him. Quick action by doctors saved his life.

On November 22, 1963, President Kennedy was murdered in Dallas, Texas. As the news was announced on television, King said quietly to his wife, "This is what is going to happen to me."

To many Americans, Dr. King was a hero. But to others, he was a dangerous man. One of those people was J. Edgar Hoover, director of the Federal Bureau of Investigation.

Hoover had run the FBI since 1924. Under his leadership, it had become an outstanding law-enforcement agency. But sometimes Hoover ran it as though it was his own police force, not the government's. He abused his power by gathering secret files on well-known Americans.

In 1962, Dr. King had complained that the FBI wasn't enforcing federal civil rights laws. Instead, King charged, the bureau was working with southern police to help preserve segregation. Hoover had never been a friend of the civil rights movement. He was convinced that the movement was run by communists. In October 1963, Robert Kennedy had given the FBI permission to put a "tap" on King's telephone.

In fact, Dr. King had rejected communism while he was still a student. Capitalism kept people in poverty, he felt, but communism stripped them of their human rights and denied the human spirit. One could not be a Christian and a communist both, he had decided.

Nevertheless, J. Edgar Hoover wanted to destroy Dr. King. When he could find no proof that King was a communist, he started prying into his private life. He had microphones planted in King's hotel rooms.

Dr. King was aware of the difference between his public image and his private humanity, as were most people who knew him well. But he worried that other people saw him only as "an angel with a halo." "I am conscious of two Martin Luther Kings," he remarked to friends. "The Martin Luther King that the people talk about seems to be somebody foreign to me." He loved to tell and listen to jokes. He enjoyed moments of laughter with young SCLC aides like Hosea Williams and Andrew Young. He was devoted to Coretta and his children, Yolanda, Marty, Dexter, and Bernice. But as he once said in a sermon, "Each of us is two selves, and the great burden of life is to always try to keep that higher self in command. Don't let the lower self take over."

Despite Hoover's efforts, Lyndon Johnson, the new president, was not interested in King's private life.

When John F. Kennedy was assassinated, African American leaders wondered what would happen to their quest for civil rights. Though Kennedy at first had not seemed to care about racial justice, he had changed. Southern senators however, were keeping his civil rights bill tied up in Congress. The new president was from Texas, a southern state. As a member of Congress, he had often voted with other southerners against civil rights bills. But recently he had said that justice and equality was "an issue that couldn't wait any longer." In his first speech to Congress as president, he said, "No memorial . . . could [better] honor President Kennedy than . . . passage of the civil rights bill for which he fought so long."

On July 2, 1964, Dr. King was at the White House when President Johnson signed the civil rights bill into law. Later, Johnson told leaders of the movement that the need for protest marches and sit-ins was over. The new law, he said, would be enough to bring justice to all Americans.

Dr. King did not believe it. It was true that much of the South was ending segregation in schools and public facilities. While places like Birmingham were grabbing the headlines, Jim Crow was dying in hundreds of other places. But King knew that this would never have happened without the pressure of direct action. The new law had nothing to say about voting rights. Even as the bill was signed, people were being killed in Mississippi trying to achieve the right to vote.

Martin Luther King shakes hands with President Lyndon B. Johnson after Johnson signed the 1964 civil rights bill.

"Freedom Summer" was a SNCC project. For several years, the students had been walking the back roads of Mississippi, quietly organizing poor country African Americans to register to vote. White students from the North had been helping out in the SNCC office. Now they were asking to share the work "in the field." This idea troubled some SNCC workers. This was a people's movement, a southern movement, a black movement. It was their own creation. They had built it from nothing at great risk to themselves. Yet some felt that it was right for whites to be involved. Didn't one of the verses of "We Shall Overcome" say "Black and white together"?

The poor black farm workers decided the matter. They wanted the white students. And so in 1964, the Mississippi Summer Project began, directed by African Americans. White volunteers from the North would help sign up voters. They would help set up schools and community centers, medical offices, and law offices. They would help organize a new political party to challenge the all-white Mississippi Democratic party.

Two of the white volunteers were Andrew Goodman and Michael Schwerner. They were based near the town of Philadelphia, Mississippi. The day after they arrived, they disappeared, along with a black volunteer, James Chaney.

The FBI was ordered to Mississippi to join in the search for the missing students. On August 4, their bodies were found buried on a farm. They had been beaten and shot. James Chaney appeared to have been tortured as well.

The public was outraged. They demanded that the killers be brought to justice. (Many African Americans however, were bitter about this response—it had taken "white deaths" to bring attention to the terror they faced every day.) The response to the murders proved to be a major blow against the Ku Klux Klan. White Americans finally saw that it was time to put a stop to the Klan and all it stood for. In December, 19 men were arrested for the murders. When a Mississippi judge threw out the charges, they were arrested again, this time under federal law. Seven of them, including a sheriff, went to prison for "violating the victims' civil rights"—specifically, the right to life.

On the day of the arrests, Martin Luther King was in Europe. He had been awarded the Nobel Peace Prize. This award is given every year to the person who has done the most to further peace in the world. Dr. King gave the prize money, $54,600, to the SCLC and other civil rights organizations.

"I am mindful," he said, accepting the award, "that only yesterday in Philadelphia, Mississippi, young people seeking the right to vote were brutalized and murdered. Therefore I must ask why this prize is awarded to a movement . . . which has not won the very peace and brotherhood which is the essence of the Nobel Prize. . . . I conclude that this award . . . is a profound recognition [of] the need for man to overcome oppression without resorting to violence."

On his way home, King met with the president. The time had come, he said, to push for a tough national voting rights law. Johnson did not agree. He could never get such a bill through Congress, he said. It was too soon after the passage of the civil rights law. The movement would just have to wait.

We've waited too long, Martin Luther King thought. If the government wouldn't help, southern blacks would have to win their voting rights themselves—through direct action.

CHAPTER 6
Selma

Legally, nothing was keeping African Americans from voting. But most southern states made it very difficult. There were tests and taxes that were applied differently to blacks and whites. Blacks were kept waiting in line all day and then not allowed to register. Individuals could sue in court if they thought they were being unfairly prevented from voting, but there were millions of such individuals. And there was always the threat of violence against anyone who challenged the system.

Selma, Alabama, was a typical southern town when it came to voting rights. Only about 2 percent of eligible African Americans were registered. SNCC had been organizing there for three years without success. In the fall of 1964, Amelia Boynton, a black Selma business-woman, asked Martin Luther King to support their cause. He agreed that Selma was where the movement would make its stand for voting rights. And he would lead it personally.

The campaign in Selma followed a now-familiar pattern. It began January 2, 1965, with a rally at Brown's Chapel. "We are going to start a march on the ballot boxes by the thousands," Dr. King said. "We must be willing to go to jail by the thousands. We are not asking, we are demanding the ballot." On January 18, direct action began when Dr. King led a march to the county courthouse. The people were marching for the vote, he declared, and the protests would go on until they got it.

Sheriff Jim Clark was "a near madman," Andrew Young remembered. "It just infuriated him for anybody to defy his authority, even when they just wanted to vote." That evening, Clark was heard raving about "the niggers." He swore to arrest them all if they returned. King decided to test his threat. The next day, Amelia Boynton led a group of marchers to the courthouse. She announced that she meant to register them to vote. Sheriff Clark shoved her out of the courthouse and down the street to his car. The other marchers were arrested too.

Four days later, a group of African American teachers marched on the courthouse. Their action risked their jobs, which were controlled by a white school board. Sheriff Clark and his officers formed a line in front of the courthouse. The marchers demanded to be let in to register.

Clark gave them one minute to leave. When the minute was up, his men drew their billy clubs and knocked the marchers down the steps. The marchers reformed their line and were knocked down again. No one was registered to vote that day. But the teachers' march was only the first by Selma's African American citizens. A court order instructed Clark to let blacks register. Clark's answer was to wear a button on his jacket that read NEVER.

On February 1, Dr. King led a group of 250 marchers to the courthouse. They were arrested. Three days later, a mass meeting was held at Brown's Chapel to protest the arrests. The crowd expected the usual speeches by southern ministers. They got more than they expected. Unknown to the SCLC leaders, SNCC had invited a speaker from New York City—Malcolm X, a popular leader among African Amercans in the North.

Not everyone in the civil rights movement was happy with Dr. King's leadership. There were some in SNCC who felt that the SCLC had built him into a larger-than-life figure, a messiah. There were even those in SNCC who were questioning nonviolence. What was the use of that strategy when their brothers and sisters were being murdered?

But if SNCC did not always agree with Dr. King, Malcolm X openly sneered at him. Of King's Birmingham campaign, he said, "The *white* man pays the Reverend Martin Luther King . . . so that [he] can continue to teach blacks to be defenseless. That's what you mean by nonviolent . . . be defenseless in the face of one of the most cruel beasts that has ever taken a people into captivity. That's the American white man."

In Selma, SCLC leaders were worried that Malcolm X might cause the people to become violent. It did not happen. On the speakers' platform, Malcolm turned to Coretta King. "Mrs. King," he said kindly, "will you tell Dr. King that I'm sorry I won't get to see him? I had planned to visit him in jail, but I have to go back to New York. I want him to know that I didn't come to make his job difficult. I thought that if the white people understood what the alternative was, they might be more willing to hear Dr. King."

The next day, a letter written by Dr. King from jail appeared in the *New York Times*. "This is Selma, Alabama," he wrote. "There are more blacks in jail with me than there are on the voting rolls. . . . We need the help of all decent Americans . . ."

Dr. King was released on bail. The meetings and marches continued. Now King expanded the voting rights drive into neighboring counties. On February 18, a rally was held at a church in Marion, the town where Martin and Coretta King had been married. State troopers were waiting outside. A mob had gathered; they attacked people as they came out of the church.

In protest against the riot, Dr. King announced that he would lead a march from Selma to the state capitol at Montgomery. The marchers would petition Governor George Wallace to end police brutality and give Alabama blacks the right to vote.

The march was scheduled to start on Sunday, March 7. It would take several days. Everyone sensed that this would be a key event for the movement. It would put the issue of African American freedom before the nation as never before.

But on Friday, Dr. King flew to Washington to meet with President Johnson. On Saturday he was in Atlanta, asking his people in Selma by phone to postpone the march for one day. He had been away from his church for two straight Sundays and needed to preach there the next day. One of his young staff members, Hosea Williams, objected to the delay. "I've got 500 people ready to march," Williams said on the phone the next morning. "They won't wait." King gave the word to let them start without him. He expected them all to be arrested, and he would join them in jail.

That was why Dr. King, like the rest of America, learned of what happened in Selma that day on television.

The marchers left Brown's Chapel for U.S. Highway 80, the road to Montgomery. To reach the highway, they had to cross the Edmund Pettus Bridge over the Alabama

River. State troopers were standing in the middle of the bridge, blocking all four lanes. "This is an illegal march," an officer shouted. "You have three minutes to turn around and go back to your church."

Nobody moved.

One minute later, the troopers charged. They clubbed men, women, and children to the ground. Then they fired tear gas at the marchers and sent them running back into Selma. Sheriff Clark was waiting there with men on horseback. Clark and his men rode through the black section of town, beating everyone they could find. By evening, 70 African Americans were in hospitals.

In Atlanta, Dr. King was stricken with grief—and with guilt for not having been there. Then he got an idea. He sent telegrams to hundreds of religious leaders. He asked them to join him for "a ministers' march to Montgomery."

On Tuesday, Martin Luther King led 1,500 marchers to the Edmund Pettus Bridge. Among them were 450 ministers, priests, and rabbis. The troopers were waiting. But this time they stood aside to let the marchers cross the bridge.

Dr. King asked the marchers to pray with him. Then he told them to turn around and march back to Brown's Chapel!

The night before, Dr. King had agreed to a compromise urged by President Johnson. He would delay the march and accept a "token victory" at the bridge. In return,

Sheriff Clark agreed that there would be no violence. The march would take place after there was time for everyone to "cool down."

Selma did not cool down. That night, three white ministers who had come to Selma for the march were attacked by four Klansmen. "You want to know what it's like to be a nigger?" one snarled. The Reverend James Reeb was hit with a club. He died two days later.

After the first riot in Selma, newspapers across the country had screamed, "Bloody Sunday!" On Tuesday, the same day as Dr. King's march, thousands of Americans had marched in other cities, some carrying signs that said, "WE MARCH WITH SELMA." Now the murder of Reverend Reeb further outraged white America.

President Johnson was reported to be "deeply troubled." He phoned Reeb's wife and personally expressed his sorrow. He sent his own plane to fly her home from her husband's funeral. More protesters poured into Selma. The following Monday, Dr. King was watching when President Johnson spoke on television before a joint session of Congress.

"It is wrong—deadly wrong—to deny any . . . Americans the right to vote," the president said. He asked Congress to pass a strong voting rights law. It would place federal officers in segregated counties to make sure African Americans were allowed to register and vote. "What happened at Selma is part of a far larger

Dr. King and his wife led thousands of marchers from Selma to Montgomery, Alabama in March 1965.

movement which reaches into every section and state," Johnson said. "It is the effort of American blacks to secure . . . the full blessings of American life. Their cause must be our cause too. It is . . . all of us who must overcome . . . bigotry and injustice. And *we shall overcome.*"

In Selma, Martin Luther King was weeping.

The Selma-to-Montgomery march finally began on March 21. Four days later, a crowd of 45,000 stood before the Alabama state capitol. Governor Wallace refused to come out to receive their petition, but the marchers could see him peeking out his office window.

"Today," Dr. King told the crowd, "I want to tell the city of Selma, today I want to tell the state of Alabama, today I want to say to the people of America and the nations of the world that we are not about to turn around. We are on the move now . . . and no wave of racism can stop us. . . . Like an idea whose time has come, not even the marching of mighty armies can halt us. We're moving to the land of freedom."

On August 6, 1965, President Johnson signed the voting rights bill into law.

CHAPTER 7
"We Don't Sing Those Words Any More"

In some parts of the South, the voting rights law led to quick changes. African Americans came together for the first time to choose candidates for public office. In Selma, Sheriff Jim Clark was voted out. In many places, the WHITES ONLY and COLORED ONLY signs were disappearing, and so were the attitudes that went with them.

But in other places, little had changed since the days of slavery. In some rural counties, many blacks could not read or write. Most were tenant farmers. They worked for white landlords who would kick them off the land if they voted. Federal officials could not be everywhere to make sure that the new law was obeyed. SNCC workers moved in to educate and organize the new voters. But many African Americans still feared white violence.

The year 1966 found Martin Luther King in Chicago. Direct action had broken segregation in the South. Now King was turning his attention to the North. Here African Americans had been voting for a century. But most big-city blacks lived in shabby, broken-down housing. Those who had money found that they could only rent or buy homes in "colored" neighborhoods. There was no Ku Klux Klan in Chicago and no WHITES ONLY signs. But blacks knew what areas of town were not safe for them to walk in. They knew what hotels and restaurants would not serve them. They knew which businesses would not hire them and which labor unions would not admit them.

Dr. King had chosen Chicago for several reasons. It had been called "the most segregated city in America," north or south. But 800,000 African Americans lived there, including some of the nation's wealthiest black citizens, and that meant power. And Chicago had a well-organized black community. They had invited Dr. King to lead a direct-action campaign for equal schools, housing, and jobs.

King and his family rented an apartment in Chicago's West Side slums. He brought in some of his SCLC staff to help in the campaign. One was a 25-year-old divinity student named Jesse Jackson, whom King had met in Selma.

Dr. King discovered that Chicago played by different rules than the South. Mayor Richard J. Daley ran a well-organized political machine, and many African Americans were part of it. Daley had been a big supporter of the SCLC when it was working in the South. But he had no wish to give up control of "his" city. He told Dr. King. that his city could take care of its own problems. He told him to go home. Even Chicago's black ministers were uncomfortable with King's presence. He had trouble finding churches where he could hold meetings.

But somehow meetings were held. King organized people in slum buildings. He listened to the stories of poverty that oppressed their lives. "We're going to organize to make Chicago a model city," he said. He met with the leaders of Chicago's toughest black street gangs and won them over to nonviolence. They agreed to work with him that summer when direct action would begin. There would be protest marches against slum housing. There would be boycotts of businesses that would not hire African Americans. These actions would be bigger than any the South had seen. But before they could begin, James Meredith was shot in Mississippi. This act changed the course of the movement.

In Mississippi, James Meredith had set out on a "march against fear." Meredith had made headlines in 1962 when he became the first African American student at the University of Mississippi. Now he planned to march

220 miles across the state to encourage blacks to register to vote. He was not a popular leader, and his march attracted little support. But on the second day, he was shot and wounded by a white man who had been hiding near the road.

On June 7, Dr. King met with Meredith in his hospital room. With them was Floyd McKissick, the new leader of CORE, and Stokely Carmichael, the new leader of SNCC. They agreed to continue the march against fear as a joint action.

That turned out to be about all they agreed on. The first day, Dr. King overheard SNCC and CORE people saying they didn't want whites on their march. At one point, King led the marchers in singing "We Shall Overcome." But when they reached the verse "Black and white together," some of the marchers stopped singing. "We don't sing those words any more," someone told Dr. King.

SNCC had broken with Dr. King the day he turned around on the Edmund Pettus Bridge. Now its people were talking about dropping the word "nonviolent" from their name. SNCC had been organizing African Americans for self-defense. They had brought armed guards on the march. They no longer used the words "Freedom now" in their rallies. Their new slogan was "Black power." King knew they meant the power of the ballot and the dollar. He also knew that some whites would think they were calling for a race war.

"If you got any notions that [we] can solve our problems by ourselves," an angry Ralph Abernathy told Carmichael, "you got another thought coming. We welcome white people." But the movement was changing. Many African Americans had come to believe that they *had* to solve their problems by themselves, because they could not depend on white support. They *had* to seize power because no one was going to hand it to them.

Dr. King knew he was being used by Carmichael. Because he was on this march, people were watching. Carmichael had raised the issue of black power to force him to take a stand. Dr. King was all in favor of black power. What he objected to was the slogan. He said that if they went around claiming power, people would turn on them and crush them. They really had power, they didn't need a slogan.

It was still Dr. King's march. All along the route, poor blacks lined the road waiting for a look at him. They rushed forward to touch him. At night, he spoke in country churches and moved people to tears with his preaching.

But it was no longer Dr. King's movement. In Canton, Mississippi, the march against fear was attacked by state and local police. The violence was worse than "bloody Sunday" in Selma. King had asked President Johnson for federal protection, but Johnson had ignored him. For SNCC and CORE, this was proof that they couldn't expect help from white America. Many whites felt that blacks did have the right to define the movement and it was clear they weren't wanted any more. They drifted away from civil rights issues. They began instead to organize against the war America was fighting in Vietnam.

The war divided people who had been on the same side in the civil rights struggle. Martin Luther King was among those who believed the United States should not be fighting in Vietnam. His stand against the war was what had caused President Johnson to desert him in Mississippi.

Dr. King would have more to say about the war in Vietnam. But for now, his concerns were in Chicago. On July 12, violence broke out on the West Side. Angry blacks smashed windows and looted stores. Mayor Daley publicly blamed Martin Luther King for the riot. He charged that King had come to Chicago to stir up trouble. In fact, it was the worst thing that could have happened for King's plans for the city. He and his staff went around the West Side talking to young African Americans, trying to get them to stop the violence. In Birmingham in 1963, people had listened to him. In Chicago in 1966, they didn't.

On July 30, the first protest march against segregated housing in Chicago was held. Whites threw rocks and bottles at the marchers. They overturned and burned their cars. The second march was held six days later. The marchers were met by a mob of screaming whites. When they saw Dr. King, they exploded. Their hate and violence was worse than anything he had seen in the South. There the mobs had numbered a few hundred. In Chicago, there were thousands. They pelted the marchers with rocks, bricks, bottles, and firecrackers. Dr. King was hit in the head with a brick. Andrew Young's car was pushed into Lake Michigan.

The city was embarrassed. Mayor Daley called for a meeting to work out an agreement on housing. Dr. King was willing. The SCLC had come to Chicago to see if nonviolence would work in the North. Some of their projects, like Jesse Jackson's jobs program, were starting to work. But they realized now that they couldn't push for all their demands at once. Chicago was just too big. Dr. King was eager for a compromise. Business leaders promised to observe the laws against segregated housing. Government leaders promised to enforce them. Labor, business, and religious groups agreed to see that the program was carried out. Dr. King agreed not to hold any more marches.

Some whites charged that Daley had sold out Chicago. Some blacks charged that Dr. King had settled for empty promises. King left Chicago on August 26. There was a general feeling that his campaign there had been a failure.

CHAPTER 8
The View from the Mountaintop

Dr. King was tired. The years of struggle had taken their toll. At home with his family, he was often quiet and depressed. Ralph Abernathy could see how troubled he was. In a sermon at his church, King spoke of his own death.

The movement was shattered. Dr. King was still committed to nonviolence and peace between the races. But people such as Stokely Carmichael were getting all the headlines. In 1967, violence broke out in 150 towns and cities across the United States as African Americans reacted against poverty and oppression. Many whites felt that King had encouraged the violence with his marches and his breaking of the law.

The movement could no longer count on the support of the federal government. In 1965, President Johnson had declared a "war on poverty." The government would create jobs and build housing in poor areas. Dr. King had welcomed the program. But two years later, all the country's resources seemed to be going into the other war, the one in Vietnam. The war was pulling the country apart. Some Americans, such as President Johnson, saw it as a war against communism. Other Americans, such as Robert Kennedy, saw it as a war against the Vietnamese people and a shame on America.

Dr. King called Vietnam "one of history's most cruel and senseless wars." In February 1967, he made a plea to "my beloved country" to stop the killing in Vietnam. The war was using up money that ought to be going to end poverty in the United States. Poor Americans were being sent to kill poor Vietnamese. What could America hope to gain from such a war? "Somehow this madness must cease," King said. "I speak as a citizen of the world [and] I speak as an American to the leaders of my own nation."

The leaders did not like what they heard. J. Edgar Hoover repeated his charge that Dr. King was a communist. This time, the president listened. He let Hoover step up his personal attacks on King. Leading newspapers attacked him. Many of his own followers criticized him. The movement had struggled hard to win government support, and King was starting to feel abandoned. SNCC had abandoned him because of his commitment to non-violence. Whites had abandoned him because of the violence of other blacks. The government was trying to destroy him because of his stand on the war. What he needed was a big nonviolent victory like Selma to rally the movement again.

It was Marian Wright Edelman who gave King the idea for the Poor People's Campaign. She was a lawyer who had been organizing poor African Americans in Mississippi and Washington, D.C. She suggested that he bring thousands of people without jobs or decent housing to Washington. They would camp out in front of government buildings and in the park across from the White House. They would shame and pressure the government into doing something about the needs of America's poor.

In Alabama, King had seen the way the poorest Americans lived. He had seen shacks with broken windows and no running water. In Chicago he had seen buildings where twelve people shared a two-room, rat-infested apartment. It was hard to get people in government to understand that there was such poverty in America. King decided to take up Edelman's idea. He would lead a direct-action campaign involving the poor of all races. Edelman assured him that they would have the support of at least one powerful government leader—Robert Kennedy, the late president's brother, and now a senator from New York.

Some SCLC people tried to talk King out of the idea. Their successes had come in fighting specific laws and customs. To attack something as huge and formless as poverty seemed like a losing battle. But Dr. King was already convinced. They had won the right to eat in any public restaurant in America, he told his people. But what good was it if they didn't have the money to buy a meal?

Money was the problem. How could he raise money to bring tens of thousands of poor people to Washington? During the fall of 1967 he traveled around the country. He talked to people who had supported the movement in the past. Everywhere he found people opposed to his plan. He should stick with civil rights, some told him. The war in Vietnam is the big issue now, others said. People will think you're trying to stir up a war of the poor against the rich, others warned.

Dr. King was more determined than ever. In Mississippi, he had visited a day-care center and seen an apple cut into four pieces for four hungry children. That was their lunch. King had to leave the room because he could not control his tears.

He announced his plan at Ebenezer Church on December 4. Beginning the following April, the SCLC would take on a massive nonviolent direct-action campaign in Washington. Poor people would come from ten cities and five rural areas. They would disrupt transportation and government operations until America responded to the problem of poverty.

The plan was greeted with anger all across the country. King was planning to take over the government, people screamed. He was planning to burn down Washington. President Johnson couldn't believe that King was bringing a "black army" against him. What president had ever done more for African Americans?

By 1968, the FBI had recorded 50 plots against Dr. King's life. Sometimes King would joke about the danger he was in. Other times he would comment, "You know, I cannot worry about my safety; I cannot live in fear. If there is any one fear I have conquered, it is the fear of death."

In February, black garbage workers in Memphis, Tennessee, went out on strike. They held protest marches, carrying signs reading I AM A MAN. When the city refused to meet with them and the police broke up their marches, the black community got behind them. They asked Dr. King to come to Memphis to organize support for the strike.

Dr. King agreed to stop in Memphis and make a speech. More than 17,000 people turned out to hear him. Their enthusiastic response reminded him of the early days of the movement. He agreed to return on March 28 and lead a march. He urged black workers to stay off their jobs that day and black students to stay out of school.

Dr. King was busy with the Poor People's Campaign. He did not take time to organize the Memphis march. Trouble broke out soon after it began. A group of African American teenagers began smashing store windows. King tried to get local leaders to stop the march. "I will never lead a violent march," he said. He and Ralph Abernathy got in a car and left. By then, there was fighting in the streets. Police were clubbing marchers, and many of the marchers were fighting back. Then the police started shooting. By the time it ended, 60 people had been wounded and one black teenager killed.

King was horrified. It was the first time anyone had been killed on a march that he led. Now what would people say about his Poor People's Campaign? Would they say that he was finished as a leader? That nonviolence itself was finished?

He decided he couldn't let that happen. The Poor People's Campaign would go on as planned. But before then, he would return to Memphis. He announced that he would lead a huge, peaceful march on April 5 and show the country that nonviolence still worked.

This time King and his aides planned the march in great detail. On April 3, they returned to Memphis. There was a bomb threat on his plane, and everyone was nervous. It was raining. Dr. King was exhausted and wanted only to go to bed. But Ralph Abernathy asked him to come speak to a mass meeting that had been arranged. "The people want to hear you," he urged. "This is your crowd."

People who were there that evening noticed how nervous Dr. King seemed, how sad he sounded. "If I were standing at the beginning of time," he said, "and God offered to let me choose what age I should live in, I would choose this, our time. Now, that's a strange statement to make, because the world is all messed up. The nation is sick. [But] only when it's dark enough can you see the stars."

He spoke of the bomb threat on the plane that day, of being stabbed in New York years ago, of how glad he was that God had let him live through the events of the last few years. "Well," he said, "I don't know what will happen now. We've got some difficult days ahead. But it doesn't really matter with me now, because I've been to the mountaintop. And I don't mind. Like anybody, I would like to live a long life . . . But I'm not concerned about that now. I just want to do God's will. And he's allowed me to go up to the mountain. And I've looked over. And I've seen the promised land. I may not get there with you. But I want you to know, tonight, that we, as a people, will get to the promised land. And I'm happy tonight. I'm not worried about anything. I'm not fearing any man. Mine eyes have seen the glory of the coming of the Lord . . ."

The next evening, April 4, 1968, Martin Luther King was shot as he stood on the balcony of his motel room. Moments before he had been preparing to go to dinner, laughing and joking with Andrew Young, Jesse Jackson, Hosea Williams, and the friend who had been with him from the start, Ralph Abernathy. He was rushed to a hospital, where he died in Abernathy's arms.

A white man named James Earl Ray was arrested for Dr. King's murder. Some believe Ray had been hired by others. There were many people who wanted to see Dr. King dead. Ray would be sent to prison for life. But to this day, some still question who was really behind the murder of Martin Luther King.

All across the nation, blacks and whites grieved for the fallen civil rights leader—and for America. His funeral was held in Atlanta on April 9. Ebenezer Baptist Church was filled. In the front of the church were Coretta, their four children, and Dr. King's parents. With them were his closest friends, those who shared his great dream and would continue working for it even though the dreamer was dead. All the leaders of the movement were there, even those who had broken with him. Robert Kennedy and his wife were there. President John Kennedy's widow was there. Nearly 100,000 people stood outside the church. Ralph Abernathy preached the funeral service. The choir sang some of Dr. King's favorite hymns. Around the world, people mourned the Reverend Dr. Martin Luther King, Jr., this man who had fought to free his people without violence, without hate.

Martin Luther King's funeral procession from Ebenezer Baptist Church to Morehouse College.

"He didn't just talk brotherhood; he was a brother," Jesse Jackson said afterward. "He didn't wish for change; he changed things."

Martin Luther King was buried in Atlanta. On his tombstone were carved the words he quoted in many of his speeches:

FREE AT LAST, FREE AT LAST!
THANK GOD ALMIGHTY
I'M FREE AT LAST

Acknowledgements

The publisher and the author wish to acknowledge that the following sources were used for background information in the preparation of this biography.

Hampton, Henry, and Steve Fayer, *Voices of Freedom.* Bantam, 1990.
Oates, Stephen B., *Let the Trumpet Sound; The Life of Martin Luther King, Jr.*, New American Library, 1982.
Schulke, Flip, *Martin Luther King: A Documentary, Montgomery To Memphis*, W.W. Norton, 1976.
Williams, John A., *The King God Didn't Save: Reflections of the Life and Death of Martin Luther King, Jr.* Coward-McCann, 1970.